HEART-SONGS

HEART-SONGS

Everyday Prayers & Meditations

SRI CHINMOY

HAZELDEN®

Hazelden
Center City, Minnesota 55012-0176

Library of Congress Cataloging-in-Publication Data
Chinmoy, Sri, 1931-
    Heart songs : everyday prayers and meditations / Sri
Chinmoy.
        p.   cm.
    ISBN 1-56838-103-4
    1. Devotional calendars. 2. Meditations. I. Title.
BL624.2.C485   1996
291.4'3—dc20   96-5149
                                                    CIP

Editor's Note
Hazelden offers a variety of information on chemical dependency and related areas. Our publications do not necessarily
represent Hazelden's programs, nor do they officially speak for
any Twelve Step organization.

CONTENTS

Spiritual leader, author, poet, artist, musician, athlete—for over thirty years, Sri Chinmoy has dedicated his enormous energies and talents to helping unlock the infinite potential of the human spirit in a quest for world peace. As an international ambassador for peace, he has guided the all-faith Peace Meditations at the United Nations for the past twenty-five years and is founder of the Sri Chinmoy Centres International, a worldwide network of 250 study and meditation centers promoting peace through various innovative grass roots programs.

Through all his writings and activities, Sri Chinmoy strives to bring forth our common aspirations to love God and to serve humanity. The prayers and meditations in *Heart-Songs* are inspired by a profound personal connection with God and a vision of the oneness of all humankind. It is Sri Chinmoy's deep desire to share these meditations with those of all faiths and creeds as part of his mission to unite us all with God and each other in a spirit of oneness and harmony.

"From our prayer and meditation we get solid peace, joy, and love," he writes. "When we pray, we ask for and receive something good and divine: God's Protection,

Compassion, Love, and Blessings. But when we meditate, we become those very things.... Then, once we become those things, it is our bounden duty to give them to our sisters and brothers in the world."

In our spiritual life, we must learn to see the Divine not only in terms of our own God but in terms of everyone's God as well. "Spirituality is not hospitality to the other's faith in God. It is the absolute recognition of the other's faith in God as one's own." A sense of humanity's true oneness is fostered by the recognition of our divine oneness, and peace and harmony in the world are the result.

The recurring theme of oneness is intended to be reflected in the language used to describe God in *Heart-Songs*. Many of the images Sri Chinmoy uses to name God are intended to reflect God's universality among various world religions. The author borrows some images from traditional language familiar to a variety of cultures. In all cases, it is Sri Chinmoys intent to banish exclusivity when speaking of God. God is not restricted to any particular creed, gender, race, nationality, or embodiment, but open to any image in which the reader finds comfort. Likewise, the prayers in *Heart-Songs* are cross-cultural, representing both Eastern and Western perspectives.

As you read and reflect upon the prayers and meditations in *Heart-Songs,* cherish and delight in the personal meaning and inner peace you find in them, using them as nourishment for your soul. But use them also as a means of developing a more global sense of your place in humanity, as a way to grow in awareness of your oneness with all peoples in a larger spiritual community. "Lasting peace must begin within the depths of the individual and from there spread in ever-widening circles as a dynamic force for world change."

Sri Chinmoys simple yet beautiful bird drawings, which illustrate each page of *Heart-Songs*, are meant to represent God's messengers of peace—the peace God offers each moment to you, personally, and to all the world as well.

—BETTY CHRISTIANSEN
Editor

Hazelden Publishing and Education is a division of the Hazelden Foundation, a not-for-profit organization. Since 1949, Hazelden has been a leader in promoting the dignity and treatment of people afflicted with the disease of chemical dependency.

The mission of the Foundation is to improve the quality of life for individuals, families, and communities by providing a national continuum of information, education, and recovery services that are widely accessible; to advance the field through research and training; and to improve quality and effectiveness through continuous improvement and innovation.

Stemming from that, the mission of the Publishing division is to provide quality information and support to people wherever they may be in their personal journey—from education and early intervention, through treatment and recovery, to personal and spiritual growth.

Although our treatment programs do not necessarily use everything Hazelden publishes, our bibliotherapeutic materials support our mission and the Twelve Step philosophy upon which it is based. We encourage your comments and feedback.

The headquarters of the Hazelden Foundation is in Center City, Minnesota. Additional treatment facilities are located in Chicago, Illinois; New York, New York; Plymouth, Minnesota; St. Paul, Minnesota; and West Palm Beach, Florida. At these sites we provide a continuum of care for men and women of all ages. Our Plymouth facility is designed specifically for youth and families.

For more information on Hazelden, please call **1-800-257-7800**, or access our World Wide Web site on the Internet **[http://www.hazelden.org]**.

J A N U A R Y

Each and Every Day

My Absolute Lord Supreme,
May my mind today and every day
Think of You only.
May my heart today and every day
Love You only.
May my life today and every day
Serve You only.
May I today and every day
Place my success-joy
And my progress-peace
At Your Compassion-Feet.

Each hour
Is a God-Smile-opportunity.
Each day
Is a man-transformation-opportunity.

Every day
Try to memorize
One God-dream-song
To make yourself divinely happy
And supremely perfect.

If you do not remain
In the desert of your mind,
Every day your heart
Will be able to weave
A beautiful, fresh, and pure
Devotion-garland
For your Lord Supreme.

May my happiness-heart
Decorate my life
With purity-flower-fragrance
   Every day.

Each day is the day
    To become
A new self-giver,
    To become
A new God-fulfiller.

You and your mind
Every day must try
To love God infinitely more
Than your mind wants you to.

Every day
I simplify my mind
So that I can
Amplify my Lord
Inside my aspiration-heart.

O seeker,
Every day start
Your life's journey
With a gratitude-heart-song.

Every day
I try to celebrate
The oneness-dream of my heart
　　Even inside
The division-enjoyment-mind.

Every day I join my heart
When it sings God-obedience-songs.
Every day I join my life
When it sings God-surrender-songs.

My soul
Every day teaches my heart
A new and soulful
Tolerance-song.

God will be satisfied with me
And God will be proud of me
Only when I climb up
    Every day
My own self-transcendence-peak.

Let us go back
    Into the world of aspiration.
Let us aspire every day
    To be worthy
Of our Lord's Compassion-Flood
    And Forgiveness-Sea.

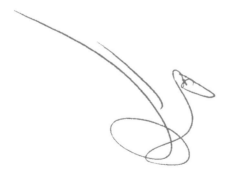

In the small hours of the morning
    Every day
My Lord Supreme comes to inspect
My heart's burning aspiration.

Never be late
For your God-appointment!
Develop invincible determination,
And every day nurture
Your Olympian dream
Of satisfying God
In God's own Way.

Every day, every hour,
Develop only one thing:
The power of dedication,
    Selfless and unconditional.

Every day
If you stand in rebellion
Against your lower self,
Your higher self
Will give you what it is:
Satisfaction-sun.

Remember,
Every divine thought
   Is precious!

Remember,
Every day the Lord Supreme
   Is gracious.

Once God becomes real to you,
Yours should be every day
    A God-preoccupied heart.

O God-lover,
Every day you must enter
    Into your heart-garden
To sow purity-seeds
And grow divinity-plants.

Ask your mind every day
To go to your heart-school.
Ask your heart every day
To sit at your soul-shrine.

Every day
My Lord Supreme blesses me
With His Compassion-Smile,
    So that I will make
A monumental attempt
    To go beyond
My daily frustration-horizon.

Every morning
Before I wake up,
My Beloved Lord Supreme
Blesses me
With His whispered Rainbow-Hopes.

If you are determined to run
        Every day
An unfaltering life-race,
Then soulfully multiply
Your heart's mounting flames.

Do not be afraid
Of the new challenge ahead
Every day.
Each new challenge
Makes your love of God
Infinitely stronger
Than you can ever imagine.

My soul is fond of planting
A new spirituality-seed
    Every day
Inside my beautiful and rich
Heart-garden.

God's Eyes bless us
　　Every day.
God's Heart forgives us
　　Every day.
God's Soul inspires us
　　And encourages us
To be God's choice instruments
　　Every day.

Every day
God puts the "Welcome" sign
On His Door.
He never uses
The "Do Not Disturb" sign.

Every day
My aspiration-heart embarks
Cheerfully and proudly
On God-pleasing adventures.

Each day is a new day.
Each new day is a new way
To see the Vision-Eye
And sit at the Compassion-Feet
    Of your Lord Supreme.

FEBRUARY

Success and Progress

You may take
Your material success
　　Carelessly.
But you must take
Your spiritual progress
　　Most seriously.

God does not want us to sound
    The success-trumpet,
But to play
    The progress-flute.

The outer success-road
    Is short
And full of apprehension.

The inner progress-road
    Is long
And full of illumination.

There was a time
When I had many goals.
Now I have only one goal:
My life's perfection-progress-goal.

If you really want to succeed
    In your outer life
And proceed
    In your inner life,
Then keep your life's dedication-door
    Wide open.

Because you have given
Your undivided attention
    To your God-life,
God is celebrating
The stupendous success
    Of your outer life
And the momentous progress
    Of your inner life.

To increase
My inner progress-delight
I have renewed my attention
To the self-discipline-life.

Your success starts
    When you become
        A determination-mind.
Your progress begins
    When you become
        A oneness-heart.

God does not mind
The slow pace
    Of my inner progress.
But God does mind
When I prefer my outer success
    To my inner progress.

God's unconditional Compassion-Eye
    Is the only force
Behind my speedy progress-life.

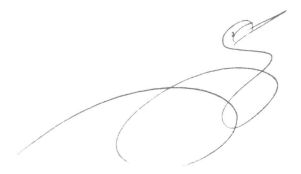

I have been on the pinnacle-peak
    Of success.
Alas! Happiness was not
    To be found there.
Now I am on the solid ground
    Of progress,
And I am all delight, all fulfillment.

My heart-progress
    Does not depend on
My life-success-performance.
My heart-progress
    Depends on
My God-surrender-blossoms.

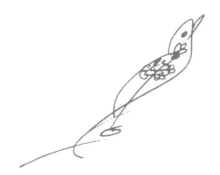

If you want success
　　In your outer life
And progress
　　In your inner life,
Then you must not slumber
　　Through opportunity-days,
　　Opportunity-months,
　　And opportunity-years.

The mind
Is fond of success.
The heart
Is fond of progress.
The soul
Is fond of God-manifestation-promises.

Meditate with greatest enthusiasm
If you want to make
    The fastest progress
In your aspiration-heart
And in your dedication-life.

A relentless determination-mind
        Is needed
To climb up the success-ladder
            Of life.
A sleepless aspiration-heart
        Is needed
To climb up the progress-ladder
            Of life.

There is always
    Plenty of room
To make continuous progress
In the seeker's aspiration-heart
    And dedication-life.

Without hope in the heart,
Without faith in the mind,
   No human being
Can ever make substantial progress.

God is so happily and proudly
    Welcoming
My success-life and progress-heart.

To achieve success
At times may not be
A difficult task,
But to make progress
Is always
A difficult task.

Success is measured
    By the outer joy.
Progress is measured
    By the inner peace.

My life's outer success
　　May please my Lord Supreme.
But my heart's inner progress
　　Definitely fulfills my Lord Supreme.

No mind-power,
No success.
No heart-power,
No progress.

If your mind has cheerfulness,
Then success is at your feet.
If your heart has soulfulness,
Then progress is inside your eyes.

I do not care for
My mind's determination-success.
All I need is
My heart's aspiration-progress.

May my mind become
A success-story of God.
May my heart become
A progress-song of God.

My mind wants
Success-procession.
My heart wants
Progress-acceleration.

You can succeed
Against all obstacles
    If you believe in
Your own aspiration-heart
    And surrender to
Your own illumination-soul.

A life of success
   Comes and goes.
A heart of progress
   Grows and glows.

MARCH

The Mind and the Heart

You have a mind
    Rich in simplicity.
You have a heart
    Rich in sincerity.
You have a life
    Rich in purity.
Therefore, God tells you
That you are rich in divinity.

I shall build my life
On my mind's determination-rock.
I shall build my life
On my heart's aspiration-mountain.
I shall build my life
In the heart of God's Compassion-Sea.

What I need
Is indomitable strength
In my mind.
What I need
Is inimitable surrender-joy
In my heart.

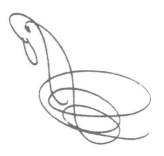

God affectionately and proudly
    Depends
On my readiness-mind
And my willingness-heart.

The heart knows
How hard it is to have peace.
    The mind knows
How hard it is to keep it.

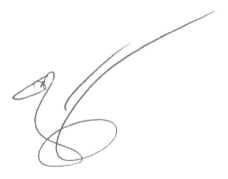

Possibility lies
    In the searching mind.
Inevitability lies
    In the self-giving heart.

What I need is
A conscious God-awareness-mind.
What I need is
A constant God-oneness-heart.

A new willingness-mind,
A new eagerness-heart,
A new surrender-life
Can and will satisfy God
    In God's own Way.

Impossibility surrenders
　　To our mind's
Self-controlled determination
　　And our heart's
God-governed aspiration.

God wants my mind to be
A reliable receiver,
    My heart to be
A reliable giver,
    And my soul to be
A reliable forgiver.

The mind is proud of itself
When it is filled with facts.
God is proud of the mind
When it is empty of thoughts.

You do not have to
    Turn your mind
To the universal mystery.
    Just turn your heart
To your self-discovery.

If you have
An understanding mind,
    And if you have
A self-giving heart,
    Then you become
A choice instrument of God,
    And of nobody else.

May my life-boat sleeplessly ply
    Between
My mind's inspiration-shore
And my heart's aspiration-shore.

A God-searching mind
And a God-loving heart
Are the dependable deputies
    Of the soul.

O my mind,
Do not retire!
Continue inspiring the world.
    O my heart,
Do not retire!
Continue praying for the world.

O my mind,
Resist temptation.
O my heart,
Invoke illumination.
O my life,
Shun insecurity.

I like my mind's
    Inspiration-smiles.
I love my heart's
    Aspiration-tears.

My mind asks me
To be the leader of everything.
My heart tells me
To be the doer of everything.

I want my heart to be
An aspiration-discoverer.
I want my mind to be
A faith-inventor.

My Lord,
I want my mind
To be a born-again believer,
My heart
To be a born-again lover,
And my life
To be a born-again server.

God's Greatness
My mind admiringly desires.
God's Goodness
My life devotedly desires.
God's Oneness
My heart self-givingly desires.

My mind's newness-beauty
    I love.
My heart's fullness-fragrance
    I need.

If the mind's sincerity
And the heart's purity
    Walk together,
Then every obstacle
    On the way
Will definitely crumble.

The mind's willingness
Is always treasured
By the heart's openness.

My Lord Supreme
Builds a peace-temple
Inside each purity-thought
    Of my mind
And each aspiration-cry
    Of my heart.

I want to go far beyond
The domain of the mind's
    So-called goodness.
I want to live inside my heart's
    True oneness-perfection.

My mind needs
Constant newness.
My heart needs
Constant cheerfulness.
My life needs
Constant fullness.
Only then
Can I ever become perfect.

I am proud of my mind
Because it is a sleepless
      God-seeker.
I am proud of my heart
Because it is a breathless
      God-lover.

The human mind searches
For something strengthening.
The divine heart longs
For something soulfully lengthening.

The mind is fond of
    God the Powerful.
The heart is fond of
    God the Merciful.
The soul is fond of
    God the Peaceful.

A P R I L

Gratitude

Each night
Before I go to sleep
I pray to my Lord Supreme
    To plant
Beautiful and positive dream-seeds
Inside my gratitude-heart-garden.

Dear to my Lord
Is my aspiration-heart.
Dearer to my Lord
Is my surrender-life.
Dearest to my Lord
Is my gratitude-breath.

In the garden of my heart's gratitude
God is performing His supreme Role
Of watching me, loving me,
And liberating me from ignorance-dream.

I wish to live every day
Between my heart's
    Gratitude-tears
And my life's
    Perfection-promise-smiles.

A gratitude-heart
Immediately knows how
To multiply life's satisfactions.

God never allows
A gratitude-heart
    To be empty
Of God's sweetest Ecstasy.

God wants from us
Only gratitude-heart-tears
And not countless
Gratitude-gift-offerings.

My Lord,
Do make my mind grateful
For what You have given me,
And my heart grateful
For what You have not given me.

My Lord Supreme,
Do give me a heart
That will never stop
Whispering soulfully:
"Gratitude."

Slowly and steadily
If you walk with gratitude-steps,
    Then lovingly and convincingly
God will come toward you
With plenitude-treasures.

Plant gratitude-seeds
   Inside your heart-garden.
Your life will be beautiful
   And fruitful
With glowing deeds.

My heart's gratitude-tears
    Will give me a new name:
        Purity-Smile.

The gratitude
Of my meditation-heart
And the Smile
Of my Lord's Satisfaction-Heart
Will forever and forever
Live together.

My life's joy will be multiplied
   A million times
If and when my heart
Becomes a sea of God-gratitude.

Gratitude is indeed always necessary.
But something else is more necessary.
　　What is it?
Unconditional and cheerful surrender,
　　Which embodies
The life, heart, and breath
　　Of gratitude.

My Lord Supreme,
You have taught me many things.
Please teach me only one more thing:
  Gratitude-multiplication.

If I am great,
    Then it is due to
My heart's gratitude-tears.
If I am good,
    Then it is due to
My life's surrender-smiles.

A heart of gratitude
Finds divine Blessings
And divine Love
All along the way.

The heart's gratitude-journey
Is always beckoned
    By the fullness
Of God's Golden Shore.

I pray to God daily
So that my life's surrender
And my heart's gratitude
    Never go on strike.

Nothing can be
More valuable and fruitful
Than to cherish
Each gratitude-breath
    Of our heart.

The golden smile
  Of Heaven
And the silver gratitude
  Of earth
Are extremely fond of each other.

A surrender-life
    Ascends.
A gratitude-heart
    Expands.

God invites only
The sleepless gratitude-souls
To participate in
His Victory-Procession
Through Heaven.

A heart of gratitude
Is a delightful responsibility
And a fruitful divinity.

You may not cherish
God's Compassion-Eye,
But God cherishes each and every
Great gratitude-breath of yours.

As every day
My life grows shorter,
    Even so every day
My gratitude-heart becomes longer.

May a sleepless
    Gratitude-heart
Be my life's
    Chief attribute.

Each time I offer
My gratitude-heart to God,
I enter into a more illumining
    And more fulfilling
        Tomorrow's dawn.

When I take a gratitude-step,
My Lord tells me
That my perfection-days
Are fast approaching.

M A Y

Peace

A mind of peace
    Loves all.
A heart of peace
    Awakens all.
A life of peace
    Satisfies all.

Power
Is meant for greatness.
Peace
Is meant for goodness.

The home of power
Is peace.
The home of peace
Is oneness.
The home of oneness
Is God's Vision-Reality.

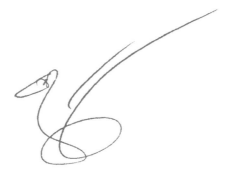

Beauty's peace-dove,
    I soulfully love you.
Humility's peace-dove,
    I sleeplessly need you.

Peace does not depend upon
My body's beauty.
Peace does not depend upon
My mind's brilliance.
Peace depends upon
My heart's fragrance.

Each and every
Peace-dreamer on earth
Must pray and pray
For peace to wake up
From its long sleep.

    Peace
Beckons the wandering mind.
    Peace
Silences the roaring vital.
    Peace
Garlands the aspiring heart.

Needless to say,
God has countless attributes.
But by far
The most significant attribute
Is peace.

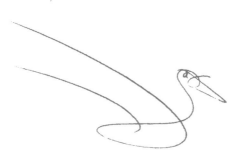

Do not stop dreaming!
One day your world-peace-dream
Will inundate the entire world.

We have one common goal:
    Peace.
But how do we achieve it?
Only through meditation
    On peace itself.

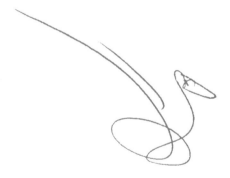

Peace will show you
The way to God.
Bliss will teach you
How to preserve God.

Where is
My mind's freedom?
It is inside
My heart's peace;
It is inside
My life's surrender.

May my life be dedicated
        Only to those
Who believe in world peace
And wish their inner lives
To be inundated with peace.

If you do not find peace
Inside your own heart,
Then you will not find it
Anywhere else on earth.

God's Manifestation-Motto
    Is so simple:
Peace within, peace without,
Peace between two thoughts,
Peace between two individuals,
Peace between Heaven and earth.

Each prayer goes up
     To God the Power.
Each meditation brings down
     God the Peace.

Peace does not mean only silence.
　　Peace is also something
Soothing, thrilling, enchanting,
　　Illumining, and fulfilling.

All the parades of the world
God has carefully watched.
Now God wants to watch proudly
    Only one parade:
The parade of the peace-flooded
    Oneness-world-family.

There is nothing more valuable
On earth or in Heaven
    Than peace,
And this peace we get
Only in our heart's oneness-delight.

Each time I pray
    I see inside my heart
        A peace-tree growing.
Each time I pray
    I see inside my heart
        A peace-flower blossoming.

O dreamers of peace, come.
  Let us walk together.
O lovers of peace, come.
  Let us run together.
O servers of peace, come.
  Let us grow together.

To think of peace
    Is not the answer.
To speak of peace
    Is not the answer.
Even to dream of peace
    Is not the answer.
But to pray for the delight of peace
    Is the answer,
        The only answer,
    To life's countless problems.

I acquire peace
Not from solitude,
But from world-servitude.

Why are you moving
From one country to another
    To find peace?
The sea of peace is just inside
Your mind's silence-sky.

In your outer life
If you long for peace,
Then in your inner life
You must become energy-action.

Peace is the perfection
    Of one's mind
And the divinization
    Of one's thoughts.

Unless your heart
Is a dance of hope,
How can your life
Be a song of peace?

A peace-blossoming heart
Is the beginning of perfection
    In human nature.

Man's soulful smile
Is indeed a perfect expression
   Of his inner peace.

Peace in my outer life
Is my perfection-smile.
Dynamism in my inner life
Is my satisfaction-dance.

Love ceaselessly struggles
     To increase itself.
Peace sleeplessly struggles
     To fulfill itself.

JUNE

*Inspiration, Aspiration,
and Dedication*

One can never outgrow
One's aspiration-heart
    And dedication-life.
One only grows and glows
    Along with them.

You are not supposed to measure
    The height of your aspiration
    And the depth of your dedication.
You are only supposed to
    Pray and meditate.
It is God who is going to measure
    Your aspiration-height
    And dedication-depth.

Beautiful are
Our aspiration-dreams.
Fruitful are
Our dedication-realities.

The beauty
Of sincere aspiration
And the purity
Of sincere dedication
Can and will
Definitely take the seeker
To his Source immortal.

Do not be afraid of going too far
With your dedication-life.
    At one point
God's smiling Eyes will greet you.

Do not be afraid of going too deep
In your aspiration-life.
    At one point
God's loving Heart will bless you.

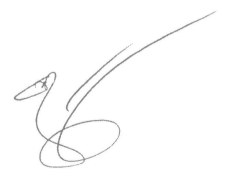

If you walk
On the aspiration-road,
Dedication-travelers
Will accompany you.

Aspiration
Is sweetness.
Dedication
Is fullness.
Surrender
Is sweetness-fullness-fragrance.

An unconditional inspiration-mind,
An unconditional aspiration-heart,
And an unconditional dedication-life
Are God-cherishing treasures.

Satisfaction within
    And satisfaction without
Come from the purity
    Of inner aspiration
And from the beauty
    Of outer dedication.

The aspiration-heart
    Began.
The dedication-life
    Has to complete.

If you are tired
    In your inner life,
Then knock at your mind's
    Inspiration-door
And appreciate the beauty
    Of your heart's
        Aspiration-house.

Since God Himself is taking the trouble
    Of examining me,
Can I not be strict
With my aspiration-heart
And my dedication-life?

My aspiration-heart
Is indeed a gift from God.
My dedication-life
Is indeed my gift to God.

My Lord Supreme,
May I find myself always
In between
My heart's aspiration-beauty
And my life's dedication-duty.

If your mind is made of
     Inspiration-dreams
And your heart is made of
     Aspiration-realities,
Then God the Pilot will grant you
     A special place
In His Compassion-Satisfaction-Boat.

He who loves God
In his outer life of dedication
Has already been loved by God
In his inner life of aspiration.

If you have a mind
    Of great intentions,
If you have a heart
    Of good aspiration,
If you have a life
    Of sleepless dedication,
Then your nature's perfection
    Cannot remain a far cry.

God does not need
Your explanation.
        No, never!
God needs only
Your prayerful aspiration
And soulful dedication.

God loves you
    For your heart's
Aspiration-purity.

God loves you
    For your life's
Dedication-intensity.

God loves you
    For your soul's
Omnipresent luminosity.

The seed
Of the aspiration-heart
And the fruit
Of the dedication-life
Can never be separated.

If you sleeplessly feed
Your heart's sacred aspiration-flame
With your meditation-peace,
Then your entire life will be
The Beauty of God's Eye
And the Luster of God's Face.

May my early morning songs be
     All inspiration-mind,
          Aspiration-heart,
               And dedication-life-songs.

My heart's aspiration-cry
    Will never fail.
My life's dedication-smile
    Will never fail.
My soul's manifestation-dance
    Will never fail.

To perpetuate
Our aspiration and dedication,
We need two things:
        A purity-heart
                And
        A sincerity-mind.

Inspiration
Is the God-journey's start.
Aspiration
Is the God-speed.
Realization
Is the God-destination.

May I be my mind's
    Inspiration-march.
May I be my heart's
    Aspiration-flight.
May I be my soul's
    Illumination-depth.

My Lord Supreme, do bless me
  With a special blessing:
I wish to remain permanently
  An aspiration-heart
  And a dedication-life.

I am not going to be satisfied
By rebuilding my aspiration-bridge
     To the Golden Shore.
I want to build a totally new bridge
     With new aspiration-flames
     And new dedication-flowers.

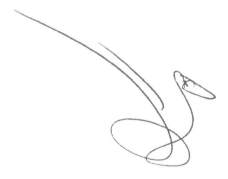

With my aspiration-heart
I sit at the Feet of God.
With my dedication-life
I become a member of God's Family.

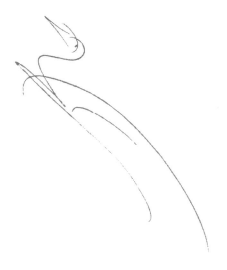

As inspiration and aspiration
Have no limits,
Even so,
Life-transformation
And God-satisfaction
Have no limits.

JULY

Be Happy and Be Cheerful

I am happy
When I pray to the secret God.
    I am happier
When I pray to the sacred God.
    I am happiest
When I pray to the compassionate God.

God tells me that
Only a perfection-heart-voice
Is entitled to
A satisfaction-happiness-choice.

The Lord Supreme
Needs only those
Who are eternally faithful,
    Sleeplessly cheerful,
And ready to follow Him
    At all times.

Enthusiasm
Rules his inner world.
Determination
Rules his outer world.
Therefore
Happiness has become
His real name.

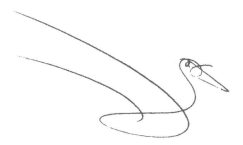

Do you want to be happy?
    Then offer to God
Your heart's permanent invitation.

Happy is the mind
　　That does not doubt.
Happier is the heart
　　That does not fear.
Happiest is the life
　　That does not surrender
　　　　To ignorance-night.

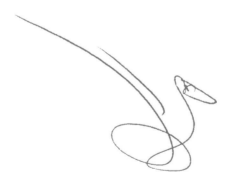

The place to be happy
God has chosen for me
With His infinite Compassion.
   The time to be happy
I have to choose for myself.
God has chosen the place:
      Here!
I must choose the time:
      Now!

God will choose your life
    Blessingfully and proudly
If you just choose your soul
    Cheerfully and unmistakably.

To conquer your mind's
    Daily frustration-fatigue
With your heart's
    Cheerfulness-light
Is always worth a try.

In the spiritual life
An eagerness-mind
And a cheerfulness-heart
Are their own immediate rewards.

If you can cheerfully accept
    The unexpected,
Then God's open Heart-Door
    Is bound to beckon you.

Your happiness-heart-flower
　　Will not fade
If you choose your soul-illumination
　　To guide you every day.

If you want to choose happiness
    In life,
Then choose willingness first.
Happiness will automatically follow.

Cheerfulness, readiness, and willingness:
    If we have,
Then we need nothing more
To please the Lord Supreme
    In His own Way.

My Lord Supreme asks me
     Only to be happy
In my inner life of aspiration
And my outer life of dedication.
     He tells me
That I do not have to strive
     To prove to Him
That I love Him and need Him.

How can a mind be happy
    If it does not look forward?
How can a heart be happy
    If it does not dive inward?
How can a life be happy
    If it does not fly upward?

Be soulful, be cheerful,
And always say yes
To your heart's inner life.
Then yours will be
The joy unparalleled.

Each aspiring heart
    Is destined to be flooded
With sweetness-happiness-fragrance.

My cheerful mind
Can elevate and even transform
Others' lives.

Willingness-seekers
Are happiness-towers
In the inner world.

If you want to be happy
Divinely and supremely,
Then you must obey your soul,
The God-representative
Here on earth for you.

God's Love-List
Has made my heart happy.
    God's Compassion-List
Has made my heart happier.
    God's Forgiveness-List
Has made me the happiest,
    By far the happiest.

Do you want to make God
    Really happy?
Then never give up your hope
Of becoming absolutely perfect.

To be truly happy
    I must live
Either inside my soul's silence-dreams
    Or inside my heart's
God-fulfilling aspiration-reality.

Two things I have
To make me happy:
    The hope that soars beyond
    And the promise that touches
        Earth-life.

At every moment
Try to make your life
A cheerful, soulful, and prayerful
    Service-song
To please God in God's own Way.

My Lord wants me
To carefully count my good points,
So that I can approach Him
    With a prayerful mind
    And a cheerful heart.

I am happy
Only when I accept
The transcendental Beauty
    Of God's Way
As my own, very own.

Real happiness
Can enter into my life
Only when I dare to think
God has not yet given up on me.

Each dedication-life
    Will eventually
Be brightened powerfully
    By inner happiness.

To be happy every day
    I open
My heart-aspiration-door
    And close
My mind-expectation-door.

AUGUST

*In the Morning
and
In the Evening*

Every morning
My Beloved Supreme teaches me
    A heart-melody
From His Compassion-Song.

Every morning I must realize
That I have the golden opportunity
    Of an unused day before me
To use in a divine way.

My morning promise:
Today I shall not fail God.
   My evening promise:
Today I shall become
An infinitely better instrument
   Of God.

Every morning
Try to greet God
With only one thing:
An ever-increasing
    Gratitude-gift.

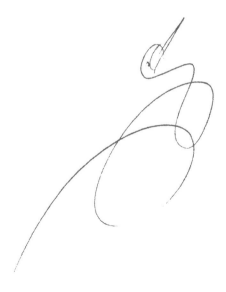

You can face the world each day
If you pray and discuss with God
    Your own life-problems
Early in the morning.

Every morning my soul teaches me
   A new surrender-song,
And every evening I teach myself
   A new gratitude-dance.

Every morning
My Lord's Compassion-Eye
    Tells me
That there is a world
    Inundated with peace,
Far beyond my proud victory
    And my sad defeat.

Every morning
My soul encourages me
And inspires me
To cross beyond
The happiness-horizon
And bring light and delight from there
To transform the face and fate
Of humanity.

This morning
I was simply amazed to see
That God was bathing
In my heart's gratitude-tears.

In the morning
God shares His Breath
With me.
In the evening
I share my dreams
With God.

The first thing I do every morning
    Is synchronize
My aspiration-heartbeat
With God's Compassion-Heartbeat.

My Lord Supreme,
May I be blessed every morning
By the magnet
Of Your Compassion-flooded Feet.

In the morning
God and I meet together
To exchange
Our Compassion and aspiration.

In the evening
God and I meet together
To exchange
Our Forgiveness and gratitude.

Every morning
God, out of His infinite Bounty,
Helps me inject my life
With the beauty of enthusiasm
And the fragrance of eagerness.

Two instruments I practice
　　Every morning:
Mind-inspiration-piano
And heart-aspiration-flute.

My morning prayer
Cries for God's Compassion.
My evening prayer
Longs for God's Satisfaction.

In the morning I pray to God
　　To illumine my mind.
In the evening I pray to God
　　To illumine my life.

In the morning I see God
Inside His Beauty's Dawn-Eye.
In the evening I see God
Inside His Compassion's
    Satisfaction-Heart.

May my morning prayer-life
And my evening meditation-heart
Grow into waves
Of sweetness-peace.

May I walk with You,
    My Lord,
Willingly, happily, and self-givingly
    Every morning.

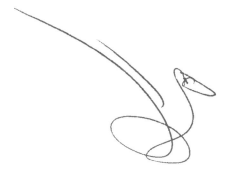

The beauty of the morning
    Inspires us.
The beauty of the evening
    Purifies us.

May each morning come to me
With an inspiration-message-light.
May each evening come to me
With a gratitude-message-light.

In the morning
    I pray
To God's Compassion-Eye.

In the evening
    I meditate
On God's Forgiveness-Heart.

My morning meditation-beauty
    Is my self-perfection.
My evening meditation-fragrance
    Is my Lord's Satisfaction.

Each morning and each evening
May I become my heart's
Rainbow-melody-flute.

Beautiful
Is my heart's morning cry.
Fruitful
Is my life's evening smile.

Greet the morning
With your heart's aspiration-cry.
Greet the evening
With your life's gratitude-smile.
At night God will grant you
His Eternity's Love
And
His Infinity's Peace.

In the morning
I reserve my heart
Only for God's Compassion.
    And in the evening
I reserve my heart
Only for God's Forgiveness.

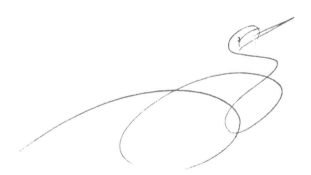

My Lord,
Do show me every morning
My sincerity's gratitude-heart-sunrise.

Every morning
I become a candidate
For my Lord's
Compassion-Forgiveness-Blessing-Light.

This morning
My Lord Beloved Supreme
    Is telling me
That before I dare to claim
His immortal Love, immortal Joy,
    And immortal Pride
        As my own, very own,
My own faith-heart-garden-blossoms
Must infinitely increase
    Their beauty and fragrance
Inside His Compassion-flooded Heart.

SEPTEMBER

*Love, Devotion,
and Surrender*

O my life's surrender-tears,
    You are beautiful,
    You are sweet,
    You are pure,
    You are perfect.
Because of you,
God every day grants me
    His Infinity's Smile.

Surrender your will
    To God's Will.
        You will see that
All your disappointments
      Will turn into
Unimaginable strengths.

Just try to love God unconditionally.
You will soon see how beautifully
    Your life's
Aspiration-transcendence-tree
    Is flowering.

Surrender now,
    And you will see,
Satisfaction will soon follow.
Aspire always,
    And remain
An eternal gratitude-student.

Love God soulfully.
God will bless your earth-pilgrimage
Richly and proudly.

When I write love-letters to God,
    He becomes happy with me.
When I write devotion-letters to God,
    He becomes proud of me.
When I write surrender-letters to God,
    He invites me to come and visit
        His Celestial Palace.
When I write gratitude-letters to God,
    He tells me to come and stay
        At His Celestial Palace
        Permanently.

Love is never alone.
Divinity's blessings
And humanity's gratitude
Always stay with love.

Infinite joy I feel
    When I see my readiness-mind
Surrender to my willingness-heart,
    My willingness-heart
Surrender to my eagerness-soul,
    And my eagerness-soul
Surrender to my Fullness-God.

My heart
Is faithfully walking
Along the path of devotion.
My life
Is prayerfully walking
Along the path of surrender.
Lo, my Lord Supreme
Is beckoning me.

If you want to win God's Heart,
Love God spontaneously
And serve God willingly.

The love-shore
　　Is beautiful.
The devotion-shore
　　Is powerful.
The surrender-shore
　　Is fruitful.

Eventually
Each and every seeker
Will run along the road
Of unconditional surrender.

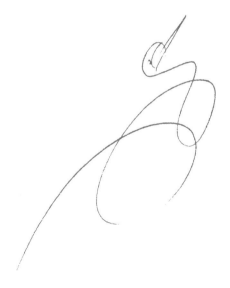

If your heart
Can prayerfully sing
Your God-surrender-songs,
Then you will be able
To breathe in freely
God's Presence-Fragrance.

My Lord Supreme assures me
That my sweetness-surrender-heart
Will be my fullness-satisfaction-life.

No love-devotion-surrender-stride
Along the path of spirituality
Can ever be too short.

A heart of unconditional surrender
    Is blessed every day
By newness-sweetness-dreams.

Each time
I surrender myself cheerfully
    To God's Will,
I see right in front of me
A free and fair highway
Leading to the Home
    Of my Beloved Supreme.

My surrender-life
And my gratitude-heart
Are being protected
Inside the heart
Of God's own Immortality.

If your life is
A constant surrender-song
    To God,
Then in God's Eye
You are infinitely greater
    Than any crowned king.

The heart that loves God
    Unconditionally
Is the heart that radiates light
    Eternally
Both in Heaven and on earth.

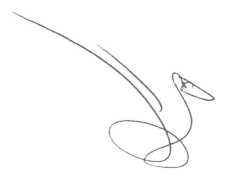

My unconditional surrender to God
Is the only strength I need
To make myself truly happy
    And fulfilled.

Surrender-road leads us
To the perfection-destination
Infinitely sooner
Than any other road.

The inner battle will definitely end
The day I turn my entire life
Into a God-surrendered song.

God not only showed me
     His Heart,
But also gave me
     His Heart
When He first saw my heart's
     Surrender-smile.

There are many boats
That sail fast, very fast,
But the heart's surrender-boat
Always sails the fastest.

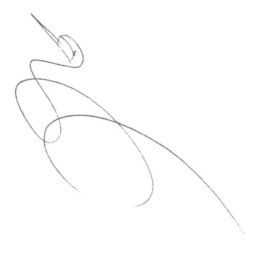

My love
Feeds God satisfactorily.
My devotion
Feeds God quickly.
My surrender
Feeds God immediately.

God gives Himself completely
To a seeker's surrender-life
And to his gratitude-heart.

I know my life
Will cease to be a problem
When I become constantly
My heart's surrender-song.

Surrender, surrender,
Surrender to God's Will!
   Then you will see
That happiness lies in your path
   Here, there, and everywhere.

God Himself came down
From His celestial Throne
    To bless me
When He saw that my life had become
A life of unconditional surrender.

OCTOBER

Prayer and Meditation

When I pray,
I cry for God's Compassion-Sky.
When I meditate,
I long for God's Satisfaction-Sun.

When I pray,
God gives me
The Joy of His Eye.
    When I meditate,
God gives me
The Love of His Heart.

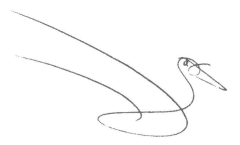

Prayers
Are the beautiful wings
And meditations
Are the soulful birds
Of my heart.

My prayer-life tells me
  How far I can go.
My meditation-life tells me
  Where I eternally am.

My prayer-hands
    Touch
God's Feet.

My meditation-eyes
    Feel
God's Heart.

When I meditate,
My Lord gives me
A heart without walls.

When I pray,
My Lord gives me
A mind with open doors.

When I pray soulfully,
My Beloved Supreme gives me
　　The capacity
To love my inner life infinitely more
　　Than I love my outer life.

When I meditate sleeplessly,
My Beloved Supreme grants me
　　The capacity
To love Him infinitely more
　　Than I love my outer life of hope
　　And my inner life of promise.

He who prays to God
    Soulfully,
And he who meditates on God
    Devotedly,
For him and only for him
His Beloved Supreme will always
    Be on duty.

Do not give up,
Do not give up!
Your prayer-life
Is your future salvation.
Your meditation-heart
Is your future perfection.
Do not give up!

When I pray and meditate,
I discover inside my heart
    A unique gift:
        Gratitude,
Which I can offer lovingly
    And self-givingly
To my Lord Supreme.

Your tearful prayers
And cheerful meditations
Are your best investment
If you want to eventually become
Rich, richer, richest
In the world of aspiration.

To accompany God
On His universal Flight,
What we need is
    The beauty
Of daily prayers
    And the fragrance
Of daily meditations.

God will hear
Your mind-prayers
If they are sincere.
God will fulfill
Your heart-meditations
If they are pure.

I feel that my prayer is perfect
Only when I pray to God
Not for His Smile,
Not for His Satisfaction,
Not even for His Compassion,
But only for Him.

The very heart
Of silence-meditation
Is the beauty
Of the soul's sunrise.

When I soulfully meditate,
I see a golden lake
Of God's Love-Beauty
    Inside my heart.

I must realize
That my God-satisfaction
Is only a prayer away.
Therefore, let me embark
On my prayer-journey
Lovingly and confidently.

God never delays
In answering our aspiring heart's
Prayerful and soulful meditations.

When I meditate,
God's Silence-Eye
   Watches me.
When I pray,
God's Sound-Mind
   Questions me.

When we pray
With a purity-mind,
Our hopeful life soars
Into God's boundless Promise-Sky.

The meditation of the heart
Cheerfully leads the mind
Out of doubt-forest.

Each sincere prayer
Has the wings to fly
    Not only from
Hope to hope-skies,
    But also from
Fulfillment to fulfillment-stars.

I have two prayers every day:
I pray to God for the early death
    Of my doubting mind
And for the everlasting life
    Of my aspiring heart.

Why do I meditate?
I meditate precisely because
My meditation proudly carries me
    To the shore I seek.

My Lord Supreme,
When I soulfully meditate,
Please bless me
With only one boon:
Grant me the ability to immerse myself
In the divine sublimity
Of my God-manifesting soul.

My prayer is to think
     Only of Him
With my purity-mind.

My meditation is to love
     Only Him
With my aspiration-heart.

When I pray,
I invoke God-Light.
When I meditate,
I distribute God-Delight.

May my morning prayer-life
And my evening meditation-heart
Grow into waves
Of sweetness-peace.

When we sincerely pray and meditate
    We come to realize
That God's unconditional Love
    Is proudly stamped
Upon our aspiration-heart
And dedication-life.

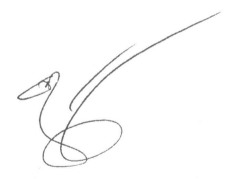

With my prayer-mind
And meditation-heart
I am going to transform my life
Into a temple of God-songs.

Today's happiness-drop
Is undoubtedly the promise
Of tomorrow's happiness-sea.
Just keep on praying and meditating.

NOVEMBER

*Transcendence,
Transformation, and
Perfection*

When self-transcendence becomes
    Your conscious choice,
The door of delight
    Will welcome you.

Patience believes in
Humanity's transformation.
Patience believes in
Divinity's Satisfaction.

Do not postpone
Your self-improvement-task.
Your soul wants you
    To make good time
And go beyond
    The limits of time.

My heart's perfection
    And
My life's transformation
    I have taken
As my soul's top priorities.

Every day
I want to be a student
Of my mind's transformation
And my life's perfection.

If we believe in our own
Self-transcendence-task,
Then there can be
No unreachable goal.

Yesterday I expected
My nature's partial transformation.
Today I demand
My nature's radical transformation.

My true accomplishments
Are nothing other than
My self-transcending songs.

You are experienced
In the art of self-transcendence.
    Therefore
God the Lover needs you
And God the Beloved utilizes you
    In a very special way.

Self-transcendence
Is the inner wealth
That pleases the Inner Pilot
More than anything else.

You may not be thinking of God
    For God's Satisfaction-Heart,
But God is thinking of you
    For your perfection-life.

Do not allow yourself
To be devoured by past mistakes,
For God is expecting from your life
A profound inner transformation.

You have all along resisted
    Temptation.
       Therefore
    Transformation
Is knocking at your life's door.

God tells me
That He will definitely
Be successful with me.
Therefore
He has been extending and extending
My life's transformation-deadline.

He is a true seeker,
   Therefore
Every day his soul inspires him
To renew his life's perfection-pledge.

God Himself has told me
That there are no speed limits
On my self-transcendence-road.

God wants from man only one thing:
He wants man to learn every day
A new song of self-transcendence.

God asks you for
Your sleepless cooperation.
God does not demand
Your immediate perfection.

My mind is thirsty for attention,
My heart is thirsty for affection,
But I am trying to be thirsty
    For perfection.

May my heart never stop dreaming
    Every night
My life-transformation-dream.

If you want to be perfect,
Then offer God your heart's purity,
    Your mind's clarity,
        Your vital's dynamism,
            And your body's alertness.

Confidence comes
Not from self-denial.
Confidence comes
Not from self-assertion.
Confidence comes
From self-sacrifice and self-perfection.

He who has
Life-transforming determination
Is already on his way
To Victory supreme.

If you accept
Responsibility's challenges,
Then your life-transformation
Will be God's top priority.

My Lord,
I invoke Your Protection-Eye,
I invoke Your Perfection-Smile,
I invoke Your Self-Transcendence-
    Whisper-Delight.

A division-mind
Will imprison you.
An aspiration-heart
Will liberate you.
A perfection-life
Will immortalize you.

My perseverance in self-transcendence
    Is a giant step
Toward my Lord Supreme.

The time to become perfect
    Is all the time.
The time to please God
    In God's own Way
        Is all the time.

A beautiful, soulful, and fruitful
　　Gratitude-smile
Is the smile of a very rare
　　Perfection-life.

There is only one dream
That will always be perfect
    In your lifetime,
And that is the dream
Of self-transcendence.

DECEMBER

*The Song of the Soul and
the Dance of Life*

God never encouraged me
To learn the world-denial-song.
    On the contrary,
God inspired, encouraged,
    And blessed me
        To sing
The world-acceptance-song
        And dance
The world-transformation-dance.

You are beautiful, more beautiful,
    Most beautiful
Only when you join your soul
    In dancing
In God's Heart-Garden.

Nothing is as eternally beautiful
    As my life's surrender-dance.
Nothing is as infinitely fruitful
    As my heart's gratitude-song.

What has God's Compassion-Eye
    Done for me?
God's Compassion-Eye has given
My body, vital, mind, heart, and soul
    Countless chances
To prepare themselves
For a perfection-satisfaction-dance
    With God.

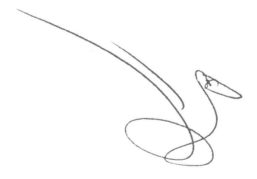

Every morning and evening
I am determined to sing and dance
    On the highest peak
        Of my sun-flooded
    Aspiration-mountain.

If you really want
To make your desire-story short,
Then start singing immediately
A long aspiration-song.

When I pray devotedly,
    God teaches me
His Perfection-Song.

When I meditate soulfully,
    God teaches me
His Satisfaction-Dance.

When I surrender unconditionally,
    God invites me to drink deep
His Nectar-Delight.

Every morning I sing and sing
In God's Compassion-Choir.
    Therefore
God has given me the capacity
    To run the fastest
Toward His golden Heart-Temple.

My Lord, my Lord, my Lord,
May my gratitude-heart sing and dance
Inside the cathedral of my soul
Every day and every hour!

Beautiful
Is the earth-illumining song
    Of my heart.

Fruitful
Is the life-transforming dance
    Of my soul.

The philosophy of the mind
    Is good.
The poetry of the heart
    Is better.
The song of the soul
    Is by far the best.

God's Fondness-Joy
Dances inside our life
     Only when
Purity's tears and beauty's smiles
Blossom inside our heart.

The happiness of the soul
    Dances only with
A surrender-blossomed heart.

Each and every aspiration-song
    Of my heart
Is bound to please
God's Illumination-Eyes
And Compassion-Heart.

If you can practice
A life of sympathy and concern,
Then God Himself will sing
His Satisfaction-Song
Inside your heart-garden.

Aspiration
Is the cry of the heart.
Realization
Is the smile of the soul.
Perfection
Is the dance of life.

May my aspiration-heart
　　At every moment
Burst with gratitude-songs
　　To my Lord Supreme.

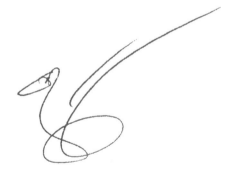

God's Pride knows no bounds
When my heart sings
A fountain-sweetness-song.

God sings for me
Many, many Songs.
But God enjoys
Compassion-Songs the most.

God will definitely bless you
With His most powerful Smile
    When you sing
Your heart-surrender-songs.

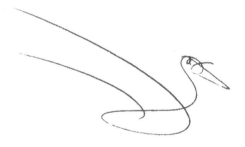

Only an aspiration-heart
Can and does sing
God's Universal Heart-Songs.

When I try to satisfy
Everybody's heart,
My soul-bird dances
Ecstasy's dance.

May my soul's dance
Be Heaven's gift to earth.
May my heart's song
Be earth's gift to Heaven.

Only one song to sing:
My heart's oneness-song.
Only one dance to dance:
My mind's surrender-dance.

Prayer
Is my heart-song.
   Meditation
Is my soul-dance.

The mind's obedience-smile
    Is beautiful.
The heart's oneness-dance
    Is perfect.

God smiles at my readiness.
God sings for my willingness.
God dances in my eagerness.

The aspiration-heart
    Always sings
God's most powerful
    Victory-Song.

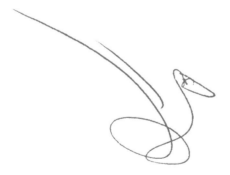

I have come to learn
That my Lord's Forgiveness-Song
 Has no final note.

My Lord,
May my life begin every day
With an aspiration-song
    And a dedication-dance.

Today I have danced
My final suspicion-mind-dance.
Today I have danced
My final hesitation-heart-dance.
Today I have danced
My final unwillingness-life-dance.